Guest Expectations in The Hospitality Property Industry

Hotels-Resorts-Inns-Bed and Breakfasts-Vacation Homes

By

Gerry MacPherson
Keystone Hospitality Property Development

Legal Disclaimer

The information presented here is based on years of experience and does contain some of our own personal feelings and practices. The contents are not the only way to operate a hospitality property but we would highly recommend looking at this information as guidelines and food for thought.

We understand you are serious about the operation of your property, this has been proven by your purchase of this book and asks that you honour our efforts by abiding by our copyright guidelines.

.

Copyright

This book and any content contained within it is not to be resold or given away for free. Copyright and illegal distribution of this book will be prosecuted. This content is solely intended for Keystone HPD members who have purchased this book. (Our lawyer said we had to put this in, hope you enjoy.)

http://www.keystonehpd.com

Table of Contents

1. How Do You See Your Property?

If you have been implementing any of the material I have shared since the beginning of this book, your business has improved. I understand that may sound like a bold statement but I know, based on years of experience that the information in this book will make your business better. I also know that you, as a hospitality property owner, bought this book to help make your business successful. So, good for you! Stick to it!

1.1 How does your property compare?

Okay, let's move on.

Here at Keystone HPD, we sat down and compiled a list of items we feel every independent hotel, resort, inn and bed and breakfast should have.

Now, these are in no particular order.

Wi-Fi

Traditional tourist demands have changed and for that reason, hospitality properties need to improve what they offer to guests by providing free WiFi. All things being equal, if it comes down to a choice between you and your competitor and you're offering free Wi-Fi, you will attract the new customer almost every time. Even the United Nations is considering making access to the internet a fundamental human right.

Other reasons to have free WiFi are:
- *It is an opportunity to collect your guest's data*
- *It is very inexpensive to set up*
- *You're meeting your guest's expectations*

Free WiFi is now available on public and private transport, in city centres, libraries, other hotels, restaurants, pubs and even churches. By you not doing this could be damaging to a business.

A sound sleeping experience

The bottom line for most room rentals is so your guests can have a place to sleep, so why not make that experience a memorable one. These are things that we have found properties have invested in to make this happen:

- All rooms have airport-grade windows (*especially if located near an airport, highway, high pedestrian traffic areas*)
- Complimentary soft slippers, (*your properties brand colour, if possible, with name or logo and non-slip soles*)

- Bathrobe(s) — nothing worse than just stepping out of the shower, hearing someone knock and then open the door while saying *"Housekeeping"*. This is the perfect time for a large comfortable bathrobe, instead of the little hand towel. *(Make them available for sale)*
- Speaking of towels *(a good size bath, 2 hand towels, and a face cloth per person)* and an extra hand towel for the ladies and sometimes men who need them to dry their hair.
- Choice of soft and firm hypoallergenic pillows
- Bed linens with minimum 300 or more thread count. 3 things to look for are;
  - *If it's Egyptian cotton*
  - *Where it's woven*
  - *The thread count (buyer beware tip: A complete sheet set with a high thread count for $100 or less is probably not the bargain you think it is)*

- Sleep Mask
- Earplugs
- A mattress that is responsive to your body (the type of mattresses you use is quite often a personal preference but if you go with mattresses similar to or from firms like the Simmons or Sealy, you should be fine. In the first and third, quarter mattresses should be flipped end to end. In the second and fourth quarters, mattresses should be flipped side to side. Depending on your occupancy they should be replaced every 3 to 7 years. As part of your routine, mattresses should be checked and cleaned at least every three months; the very last thing a guest wants to see is any

staining and stay away from the plastic-coated mattress as they have in hospitals. All hospitality properties should have at the very least a mattress protector of some sort on their beds, preferably the most absorbent. It is also not a bad idea to have an additional soft layer of absorbent material such as a wool-rich blanket used beneath a mattress protector. This can act as a final vapour barrier.

Blackout drapes

This is something I feel is a must for hospitality properties. Whether you're trying to get a few hours' sleep in the afternoon or you're feeling a little restless at night, having a dark undisturbed place to sleep can help you get to rest you need.

Adequate power outlets

I travel with a smartphone, a tablet, an iPod and a camera and based on what I've seen, I am not the only one. The thing they all have in common is that they have to be charged so I am still surprised when I walk into a hospitality property room and find only one or two outlets for guests and more often than not they are hidden behind the bed. An ample number of easy to access power outlets strategically placed above the desk, table, and night stand should be a standard in rooms.

A good luggage rack

Whether the rack is out in the open as soon as I walk in the room or a closet for me to take out either way, is okay with me as long as there is one. This has nothing to do with the possibility of little creatures crawling into my suitcase, although that could be a concern to many, I don't appreciate the stress on my back.

Coffee maker

A room with a good coffee or espresso machine as well as a hot water machine or kettle for tea. It is so nice to start a relaxing morning knowing you don't have to go to the dining area for your first caffeine jolt. Another nice idea is to have soup packets available.

My wife and I have a great memory of being on the road for a week in Ireland and not feeling like going out for dinner, instead, we sat in front of our hotel room's window, in bathrobes, eating noodle soup. It was perfect, and we still talk about it as a great memory.

Corkscrew

This may seem like a no-brainer but very few properties have corkscrews and wine glasses in their rooms. Most airlines do not get excited at the idea of passengers carrying their corkscrews so this is where hospitality properties could pick up the slack and also put their logo on them.

Easy to operate showers

I have walked into hospitality property rooms and saw showers that I was sure came straight from Star Trek. It's wonderful to have so many options but if I don't have the time or the desire to study the manual, is it too much to ask to have a simple on/off option? I'm a simple man from a simple time, so easy-to-understand step-by-step instructions are greatly appreciated.

A mini oral hygiene kit

I try to be organized, but there have been times when I forgot my toothbrush or toothpaste and didn't realize it until I arrived at a hospitality property. Mini kits with an inexpensive toothbrush, toothpaste and maybe a sewing kit would be immensely appreciated.

Free bottles of water

It doesn't have to be a fancy bottle or high-end water, just something to quench the thirst. And it is great when these bottles are replaced daily.

Ornamental bed pillows or cushions

When I first started travelling, walked into a room and saw a decorative pillow or a stuffed animal, I used to think *"That's nice"* now I think *"Has that ever been washed?"* I'm afraid the answer to my question in most cases is no. I want to know that there is a least a chance that the pillows are clean and as far stuffed animals go, leave them in the box and not my room.

Closet hangers

There is a real good chance I am not going to pay your room rate, just to steal your hangers and those who do wish to steal them are probably few and far between.

Since I have been travelling professionally for over two decades, the idea of travelling light is important to me. However, I do bring nice things with me and I like to hang them up so they don't get wrinkled. It drives me crazy to open a closet door to find a hanger that doesn't come off the bar or a variety of plastic hangers. A good rule of thumb is to have six wooden hangers per guest. I want to feel welcome at a hospitality property and not like a possible thief.

Computer / printer

Even in this age of advanced technology, there are times I need access to a computer and printer.

Information packages

When, I arrive at a new property one of the first things I do is look at their information packet. These are the type of things I look for:

- *Property history*
- *Property rules and guidelines*
- *Menus*
- *Room service menu (if applicable)*
- *Eating establishment options within the area*
- *Phone procedures (for international travellers)*
- *Local attractions*
- *And any other relevant information*

So, how do you compare? Maybe you're looking at our list and saying *"No problem, I have all that covered"* or you might be saying *"I never thought of those"*. Either way, as professional travellers, these are the type of things we look for, and we know your guests will appreciate.

If you have other must-haves I should add to the list, please let me know.

2. How To Become Your Own Guest

Several years back, I was approached by an acquaintance who was looking for some advice. He was a very smart businessman, an entrepreneur who had many business ventures on the go including being a business realtor.

He was very analytical and focused on the bottom line, but he came across one business for sale, an independent hotel, and was intrigued.

He thought it had a lot of potential so, he bought it himself.

He calculated the cost of running the business; the occupancy rate required to start making a profit; and a marketing strategy. Within no time, the business was coming to his door.

A year later, he contacted me and asked to meet. He told me he was getting a fairly steady stream of business, but very little or no return business.

I asked him *"What are your guests telling you on their comment cards or surveys?"* he told me he did not have comments cards available and that he had never done a survey.

I then asked, *"Are your staff trained to ask for complaints?"*

He told me that aspect was not covered in training, and then he admitted, there was very little training for any of his staff.

I suggested I could check in and stay a night and then report to him with what I found.

His staff did not know me and thought I was just a walk-in looking for a room. The receptionist was friendly enough but while checking me in was chatting with one of the housekeepers.

When I asked for a recommendation for a place to eat, she said: *"There is a take-out food place across the street"*.

That was her only suggestion and ended the conversation there.

The room was nice enough, nothing fancy but it seemed clean.

After taking a little time to do an inspection, I found that the window had been nailed shut; there was a hair in one of the bathroom glasses; when I turned on the radio I found it was very loud and set to the country station; and that the mattress had stains on it.

My sleep was restless, not only because of the stains on the mattress but it was uncomfortable and the pillows were flat.

The breakfast was passable, but nothing exciting and the checkout was fast with very little conversation and no one asked about my stay.

When we met later that day, the owner wanted to know everything but the first thing I said to him was, *"When was the last time you stayed in your hotel?"* and he said, *"I've never stayed in my hotel".*

I recommended that he do that before we have our chat.

He took my advice and a couple of days later he walked up to the front desk and told his receptionist that he would like to check in and be treated like a regular walk-in customer.

Of course, it was a little harder for his employees to think of him as a regular guest, but he was able to get an idea of what his guest experience.

He invited other acquaintances to check into his property and report back what they found and over the next few months, he stayed in every room, taking time to go through them and every corner of his property with a fine-tooth comb.

He and his employees took the time to create a fully functioning operations manual and all his staff were trained.

His return business increased dramatically and his revenues increased by 47% in 12 months.

This is an exercise that many hoteliers I've met over the years have told me they would like to do but cannot find the time.

My response is always been the same *"This is your business, your livelihood, you will have to know what's going on. Make the time".*

Small to medium independent hotels, resorts, inns and bed and breakfasts have so much to gain from this advice. If you have not taken the time or not thought of staying in your property as an option, it's a good idea to put it on your calendar much sooner than later. A different perspective can surely open your eyes.

2.1 Hotel site inspection checklist

(can be modified for any hospitality property type)
Location:
    How far from public transportation?
    Is it located in a *safe* area?
    Does the hotel provide transportation to and from the airport?
    Are there other hotels located nearby?
    Does the appearance of the hotel look pleasing?
    Is the hotel attached to a shopping area?
    Is the hotel near a shopping area?
    Is the hotel located downtown?

Parking:
    Space
    Paved
    Distance from entrance
    Motorcoach parking
    Security
    Lighting

Green Area:
    Trees
    Walking area or paths
    Children play area
    Lighting

Guest Rooms:
    What is the rack rate?

Corporate rate?
Any special rates
Weekends, holidays, seasons?
Are guest room furnishings adequate and well maintained?
What amenities are available in each room?
Are rooms well-lighted?
How many guest rooms can the hotel commit to a meeting?
Are there designated non-smoking rooms?
What are the check-in times and check-out times?
Is there a concierge level and what are the rates?
Are some rooms set aside for the disabled?
The room was clean
The furniture was in good condition

Décor:

The bed was comfortable
The lighting was adequate
The TV had good reception
The room had a nice view
The room was quiet
Housekeeping kept the room in order
Housekeeping services
Heating/cooling within the room
Extra pillows
Extra blankets
Can I easily control the room air

Lobby Area:

Is the lobby attractive and spacious?
Is the lobby area well-furnished?
The hotel had my reservation

Is the front desk well-staffed?
The check-in staff was polite
Are there long lines for check-in and check-out?
Are bellmen readily available?
Someone was available to assist with my luggage
Are elevators easy to locate, fast, clean?
Is security apparent?

Banquet Room/Food and Beverage:
What are the room sizes and how many people can be seated?
How many places will the property set up beyond the stated
number of   guests?
How far is the banquet room from the kitchen?
When does the property need a final guarantee?
Does the property have ample restaurants?
Room service was prompt
Will the hotel set up special morning coffee areas for guests?
Is the restaurant well-staffed?
Is room service available and what are the hours?
Will the property food and beverage outlets accommodate
special requests?
Menu Variety
Value for price paid
Promptness of service
Quality of service
Quality of food
Quality of beverage
The restaurant was clean
The food was reasonably priced
The menu offered foods that I like
The quality of the food was good
The quality of the service was good

The staff was polite

Overall, how was your stay?

Meeting Rooms:

How many meeting rooms does the hotel have?

How large/small are the rooms?

What is the capacity of each room for different sets (e.g. theatre, school room, banquet)?

Does the property have enough inventories?

What does the property supply?

What will the planner have to order?

Do the meeting rooms have obstructions?

Are air walls soundproof?

Is the meeting rooms wired for sound?

Is there an in-house A/V company?

Where are the restrooms, phones, etc.?

Can I easily control the room air?

Security:

Does the hotel have an emergency plan?

Is the fire exits well-marked?

Other:

Is there a health club? If so, what are the charges?

Is there parking and what are the charges?

Does the hotel comply with Americans with Disabilities Act (ADA) requirements? (or similar requirements)

Are there babysitting or daycare services offered?

Exercise Area:

Gym equipment

The pool was adequate
Showers
Sauna
Hot Tub
Jacuzzi
Are towels available?
The game room was adequate

8.2.2 Guest room checklist

Below the room checklist that should be checked daily

Doors
Exterior washed/dusted
Interior washed/dusted
Peeling paint/other damage
Does not open/unlock easily
Weather-stripping needs replacement
Room numbers missing

Bedroom
Floors vacuumed/cleaned
Walls cleaned as required
Ceiling cleaned as required
Carpet has holes/cigarette burns
Carpet requires a steam cleaning
Walls damaged
Walls require repainting
Ceiling damaged
Ceiling requires repainting

Windows

Exterior washed

Interior washed

Sills cleaned/dusted

Clean curtains/drapes

Broken/missing, require replacement

Torn/missing screens

Curtains/drapes require mending

Beds & Linens

Clean/fresh linens

Clean/stain-free bedspread

Hide-a-way bed linens are fresh

Sagging — require replacement

Bedspread requires mending

Furniture & Furnishings

Furniture polished/dusted

Waste-basket/ashtrays emptied

Sanitized glasses in place

Missing hangers replaced

Disposable items discarded

Standard guest room amenities replenished

Mirrors cleaned

Phone disinfected and earpiece cleaned

Television dusted, including top and back

Thermostat set per house policy

Lampshades dusted

Burnt out lights replaced

Drapes properly hung

Disinfectant spray used

Excessive scratches on furniture

Torn upholstery
Missing knobs on dresser/desk
Mirror needs replacement
The TV needs adjustment/repairs
Phone requires repairs
Light switch/plate broken
Wall sockets not working
Broken/missing lampshades
Smoke detector not functional
Thermostat not functional
Air conditioning filters require cleaning
Curtain rods broken

Check for Guest Belongings
Under-bed
Inside drawers
Back of bathroom door
Bathroom cabinets

Additional Dusting Performed
All woodwork
Picture frames
The shelf above clothes hangers
Door Sills
All ceiling/wall vent grills
Cobwebs removed

Bathrooms
Tub/Shower cleaned & disinfected
Tiles scrubbed
Toilet cleaned & disinfected

Sink cleaned & disinfected

All chrome taps polished

Inside of shower curtain wiped clean

The shower rod wiped clean

Shelving wiped down

Ceiling cleaned as required

Walls cleaned as required

Floors washed

Fan vent grill free of dust accumulation

Standard guest room amenities replenished

Fresh towels & bathmat supplied

Soap & shampoo provided

Sufficient facial & toilet tissue provided

Door damaged

Shower stall rusted

Loose tiling around the tub

Leaking taps/faucets

Loose toilet seat

Toilet — mechanical problem

Caulking around tub/fixtures deteriorating

Noisy fan

Fan not working

Walls/ceiling needs painting

The shower curtain needs replacement

Loose floor tiling

Mirror needs replacement

2.3 Quality of service assessment checklist

Quality Dimension Samples of questions to ask

Tangibles:
- The appearance of physical facilities, equipment, personnel, printed and visual materials
- Are facilities attractive, clean and visually appealing?
- Is provided equipment and facilities in good working order?
- Do staff give a neat, professional appearance?
- Are materials and written communications associated with the hospitality property brand visually appealing and easy to understand?
- Is technology and equipment up to date?

Reliability:
Ability to perform promised service dependably and accurately
- Is service performed right, to the required standard, the first time and as promised?
- Is the level of service the same at all times of the day and for all members of staff?
- Are all services/ facilities available as promised?
- Is there dependability in handling guest problems?
- If a response or action is promised within a certain time, does it happen?

Responsiveness:
Willingness to help guest provide prompt service
- Is service provided at times and places it is needed?
- Is service provided with minimum inconvenience to the guest?
- Do staff show a readiness to respond immediately to guest requests?
- When there is a problem, do staff respond to it quickly and with empathy?

- Are guest needs anticipated and acted upon?
- Are guests kept informed about relevant changes?

Competence:
Possession of required skill and knowledge to perform service
- Can staff provide service without fumbling around?
- Are materials provided appropriate and up to date?
- Can staff use technology quickly and skilfully?
- Do staff appear to know what they are doing?

Assurance:
The ability to instil confidence and perceived security in all interactions the guest has with the establishment
- Do staff and management instil confidence in a guest?
- Do guests feel safe and secure on the premises?
- Are staff consistently courteous?
- Are staff able to answer guest questions about the Hotel's facilities?

Courtesy:
Politeness, respect, consideration and friendliness of contact personnel
- Do staff make eye contact and smile when a guest approaches?
- Do staff greet first?
- Do staff give guests their undivided attention (free of interruptions or distractions)?
- Do staff attempt to address the guest by name?
- Do staff members have a pleasant demeanour?
- Do staff refrain from acting busy or being rude when guests ask questions?

- Are those who answer the telephone considerate and polite?
- Do staff observe consideration of the property and values of guests?

Empathy:
Making the effort to know guests and understand their needs.

- Do staff and management understand the needs of different guests?
- Do guests receive individual attention?
- Do front-line staff recognize regular guests and address them by name?
- Do staff and management listen to guest's problems and demonstrate understanding and concern?
- Are various options to a particular query clearly explained?
- Do staff have the guests best interests at heart?

Security:
Freedom from danger, risk, or doubt

- Is it safe to enter the premises and to use the property's facilities?
- Are documents and other information obtained from the guest held securely?
- Are use records of guests safe from unauthorized access and use?
- Can guests be confident that the service provided will be done correctly?

Access:
Approachability and ease of contact.

- How easy is it to talk to a knowledgeable staff member when guests have a problem?
- Is it easy to reach the appropriate staff member...
    - *In person?*
    - *By telephone?*
    - *By email?*
- Is management easily accessible to the guests?

Communication:

Listening to guests and acknowledging their comments; Keeping guests informed in a language they can understand.

- When guests contact the service point, will the staff person listen to their problem and demonstrate understanding and concern?
- Can staff explain clearly the various options available to a particular query?
- Do staff avoid using technical jargon when speaking with guests?
- Are guests informed in a timely fashion when there are problems that could affect them or the hospitality property's services?

2.4 Exhibit checklist

Exhibit Hall:

Secure floor plans of the hall: note entrances and other obstructions.

What is the total square footage of floor space?
What are the ceiling heights?
How many booths can fit into the allotted space?
Where are the electrical outlets?

Where are the loading/unloading facilities?
Are there any storage facilities?
How close is the hall to the meeting rooms?
Where are the restrooms?
What security will be needed?
What are the insurance considerations?
What equipment will the property provide?
What equipment do users have to contract for?

Labour:

Rates for:

- *Electricians*
- *Carpenters*
- *Decorators*

Exclusives
Limitations
Can exhibitors bring in their own material(s)?
What are the union requirements? (if applicable)

Services:

Storage
Booth cleaning
Security
A/V equipment rental
Phones
Who provides pipe and drape?
Will the hotel provide tables and chairs?
Delivery to hall/booth

Access:

Who has access?

Hours of operation
Hours of set-up
Hours of dismantling
Off-hours admission
Theft reporting
Access to show *(open versus registrants only)*

Planner Responsibility:
Number and size of exhibit booths
Overall decor, colour scheme and theme
Rental charges to exhibitors
Number of booths permitted each exhibitor
Booth versus table-top displays
Type of product or service on display
Signs
Length of show

3. Is Your Hospitality Property Accessible?

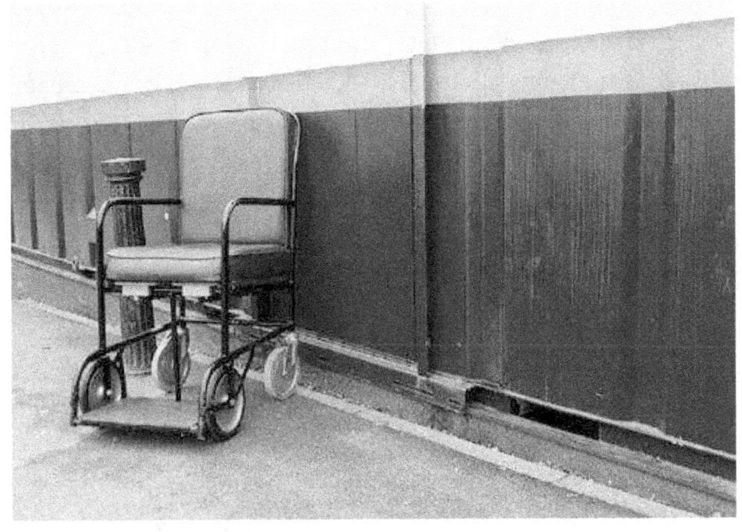

Now, I understand rules and guidelines will vary depending on where you're from, but I also know if I were to share all the rules and regulations worldwide, this chapter would probably be a couple of thousand pages long. For simplicity's sake, I am going to refer to the 2010 ADA (Americans with Disabilities Act) Standards for Accessible Design, updates.

3.1 Is your hospitality property accessible?

Just having a couple of rooms allocated accessible does not necessarily mean your property is compliant with your country's rules. Rules can be updated and any new renovations in a room might make elements of that room inaccessible. I have attached a link to the 2010 ADA Standards for Accessible Design in the resource section for you to study if living within the United States, and to compare with your own countries guidelines and regulations outside the U.S.

Since the United States still uses the imperial system for measurements, I have also included a link to an imperial/metric conversion chart.

Hospitality properties should ensure they have all the required elements necessary as an accessible property; here are tips on what to look for:

- *An accurate and reliable reservation system to provide persons with disabilities the ability to reserve rooms with accessible amenities*
- *A sufficient number of accessible rooms, including rooms with communication features (see the included Guest Room Requirements)*
- *Amenities that are provided in inaccessible guest rooms must also be provided in accessible guest rooms (for example, if vanity counter top space is provided in inaccessible guest room bathrooms, then comparable vanity spaces must be provided in accessible guest rooms)*
- *Distribution of accessible rooms among the various classes of your accommodations (what you should consider includes; room size, bed size, cost, view, fixtures such as hot tubs and spas, non-smoking/smoking, and the number of rooms provided)*
- *Accessible sleeping rooms with roll-in showers as required by the standards*

- *Accessible fire alarm or other emergency warning system for individuals who are deaf or hard of hearing*
- *Accessible pathways approach protected from the elements and turning space for wheelchairs*
- *If carpeting is provided, ensure it is low-pile, tightly woven and securely attached*
- *Handles and dispensers that can be operated easily with one hand*
- *Tub and shower seats that can be securely attached*
- *Accessible dispensers and operating controls within reach*
- *Accessible light switches, thermostats, drapery wands and door security hardware*
- *Accessible sinks and toilets with grab bars*

As owners of hospitality properties, you should make sure you're compliant with your country's accessibility rules and regulations. This could protect you from liability and will increase your marketability to persons with disabilities.

Alright, I'm leaving you with lots to do. To help, I have included charts and images with guest room and toilet requirements. When you or your acquaintances are going through these checklists — make sure, to be honest, and don't make excuses. If you take this exercise seriously your property can't help but improve.

Accessible guest room

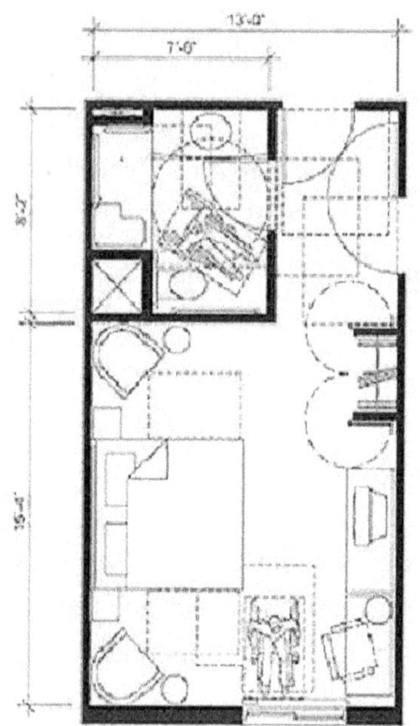

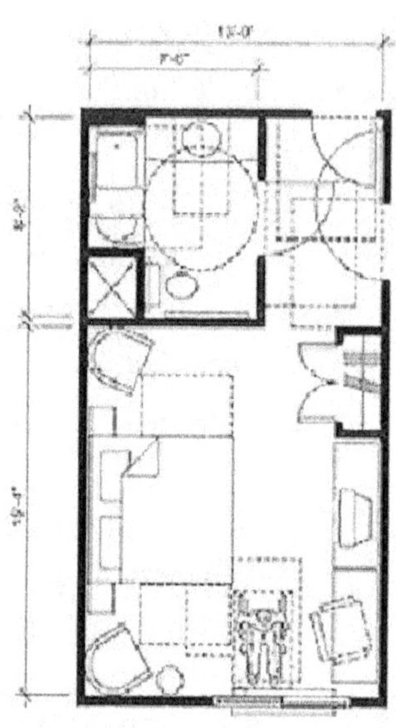

Accessible guest room requirements

Table 224.2 Guest Rooms with Mobility Features

Total Number of Guest Rooms Provided	Minimum Number of Required Rooms Without Roll-in Showers	Minimum Number of Required Rooms With Roll-in Showers	Total Number of Required Rooms
1 to 25	1	0	1
26 to 50	2	0	2
51 to 75	3	1	4
76 to 100	4	1	5
101 to 150	5	2	7
151 to 200	6	2	8
201 to 300	7	3	10
301 to 400	8	4	12
401 to 500	9	4	13
501 to 1000	2 percent of total	1 percent of total	3 percent of total
1001 and over	20, plus 1 for each 100, or fraction thereof, over 1000	10, plus 1 for each 100, or fraction thereof, over 1000	30, plus 2 for each 100, or fraction thereof, over 1000

Table 224.4 Guest Rooms with Communication Features

Total Number of Guest Rooms Provided	Minimum Number of Required Guest Rooms With Communication Features
1 to 25	2
26 to 50	4
51 to 75	7
76 to 100	9
101 to 150	12
151 to 200	14
201 to 300	17
301 to 400	20
401 to 500	22
501 to 1000	5 percent of total
1001 and over	50, plus 3 for each 100 over 1000

Accessible guest room toilet

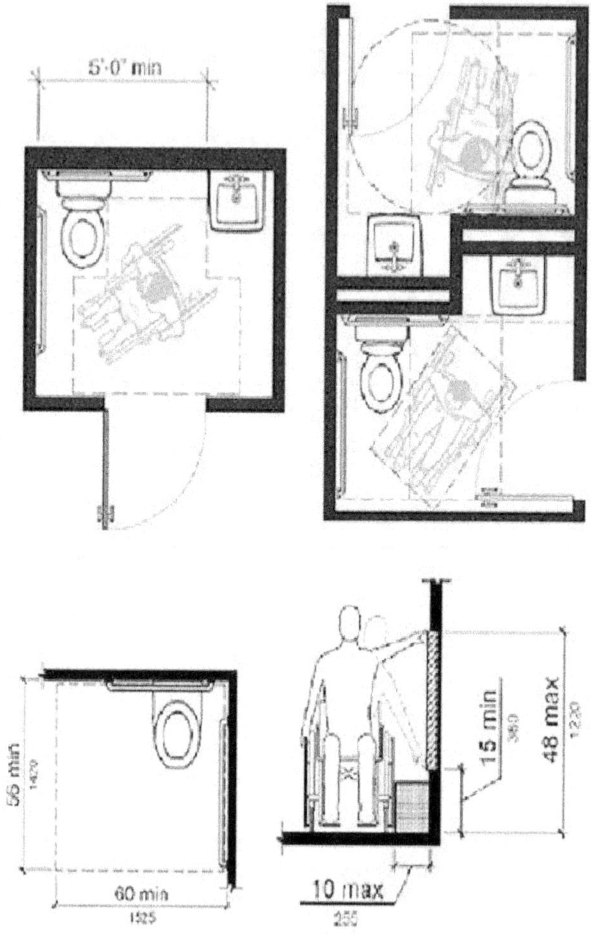

4. Is Your Restaurant Meeting Its Potential?

If you have a restaurant and you're only catering to your property guests, then you're leaving money on the table. You might believe you have a very good restaurant, in fact, you might believe you have a great restaurant but without good local patronage, how would you know for sure. Hospitality property restaurants normally are not on the radar of potential customers when they are looking for a place to eat. Traditionally, hospitality property restaurants have a difficult time attracting locals.

4.1 What can you do to improve your chances?

I'm going to share some ideas that have worked with many hospitality property restaurants.

- *Consider trying a new name, identity and theme for your restaurant, and promote it to the local market separately from your property.*
- *Use social media and the local press to market your restaurant. You can contact journalists from local publications and invite them for a meal on the house in return for a review.*
- *Set up a competition in the local press and online, with a prize of a meal for four with wine. The contest will cost very little and if done right can be very effective.*
- *Offer a choice of menus; for families and vegetarian options.*
- *Highlight what makes you stand apart from your competitors, other restaurants. (Is it better service, bar and lounge areas to relax before and after a meal, space for kids to run around, easy parking, a rural getaway).*
- *Create a separate website for your restaurant.*
- *Be sure your restaurant is listed in the local tourist & travel guides.*
- *A great way to keep both your staff and customers excited is to offer menus that are seasonal and that are changed regularly.*
- *Use local suppliers and declare this in detail on your menu, your website and any marketing you do. Local suppliers will support you by advertising your property verbally.*
- *Make sure all local hotels have your menus and it would also be very useful to invite the head concierge or front desk receptionists for a free meal. We talked about cross-promoting earlier and know they will be more likely to recommend your restaurant to their hospitality property guests if they can talk from first-hand experience.*

- *Get your local businesses involved. Contact and invite the local business associations in for a familiarisation dinner. Offer a time-limited discount to two or three of the largest nearby employers. This could be a 20% discount to their employees, which they could promote in-house and by putting a time limit on the discount, you encourage people to use it sooner rather than later.*
- *You could offer theme nights, music events, wine weekends and private special events.*
- *Make sure each guest receives a warm welcome and that you and your employees go the extra mile to make it a great experience.*
- *Ask for your customer's opinions. Talk with them and make feedback cards available.*
- *Make sure to incorporate a method to gather all new customer data information such as e-mail addresses and add them to your newsletter list. Newsletters could be monthly news/recipe/events letters.*
- *Market your restaurant as a destination and attract foodies who are looking for a weekend away and offer reduced room rates for diners who stay over.*
- *Offer gift certificates to local charities, school or social events. This can work well for your branding.*
- *Make your restaurant easy to find. Good well-illuminated signage and easy-to-find parking are important if you don't want your potential customers to get lost or frustrated and find one of your competitors instead.*
- *Make sure you have an organizational strategy in place and that everyone knows exactly what their duties are.*

You have to live up to your promise — there is no sense in trying any of the strategies I have mentioned if the quality of service is going to be subpar. I had mentioned before that a restaurant inspector I know told me the first two things he looks for are whether the toilet is clean and the lettuce is fresh.

4.2 Last word of advice

Don't try to be everything to everyone, find what you're great at and do it to the best of your ability. Whenever I see a hospitality restaurant or dining area and hear it is empty most of the day, I see revenue floating out the window.

5. How To Get Endless Referrals

As an independent hotel, resort, inn or bed and breakfast, a very effective way to grow your business is through
referrals. Unfortunately, referrals do not happen effortlessly. Yes, you might get the odd referral, but if you want your business to grow you have to both earn and ask for them.

Let's begin by talking about how you can earn great referrals from your guests. You can start by giving them an experience they will remember, you want to *WOW* your guests.

Here some ways you can amaze or wow your guests:

Show your interest by really listening to them.

Ask the right questions during the check-in, in your restaurant, at the bar and listen to the answers but don't make it obvious.

For example:

- *Have newspapers available at the front desk and ask what paper your guest likes to read.*
- *Keep track of the drink they have if in your restaurant or bar.*
- *Ask if they have a favourite coffee or tea.*

These are questions or observations that can be made during casual conversation and without being obvious.

Why?

All these answers can be recorded in your guest's profile to be used later.

During turn-down service, leave their drink of choice in their room as a nightcap. If possible, have their favourite coffee or tea for them for the next morning and the coffee machine timed to start brewing the same time as their wake-up call. Have their favourite newspaper delivered to their room five minutes after their wake-up call; just a light knock at the door and leave it.

Now, you might not be able to fulfil all these wishes and that is alright because the guest would not know it was happening but imagine the surprise if you can do one or any of these.

Have the appropriate software system

Ensure your guests' 2nd, 3rd or 100th visit is as good as their first. Have systems in place to guarantee you can have the same degree of service consistently. A quality check-in system should enable you to build a profile for the guests that you can use for every visit. The upfront cost for such a system may be high but if used properly you will recoup your investment with returning guests in no time.

Hire the right employees

Compassion cannot be taught, you can't give employees the desire to bend over backwards for customers. Hire employees that can show compassion to your guests. Have the appropriate systems and tools in place for them to deliver the first-class service. Empower them with confidence and authority to deal with complaints promptly.

Know your guests

Learn your guest's names and use them. Also, teach your staff to recognize and remember loyal guests. This will form an immediate sense of hospitality that they'll certainly find flattering.

After the check-in

Once you have given decent time for your guests to settle in their room, the front desk should phone the guests to make sure everything is in order and acceptable. During this call, you will be able to ask if any additional requests may have been forgotten during check-in.

Be available

Be on hand at your property and have personal contact with your guests to build rapport and confidence. Get to know and listen to your guests. They're far more likely to tell you what they want if they know you and that would encourage them to come back. If you know your guests, it's easier for you to anticipate their needs and deliver them consistently to keep them satisfied.

Be flexible

Don't be so constrained by your own rules that you can't extend breakfast for a guest who may wish to sleep in or to extend a check out if someone has a late flight. Is this that big a problem if it means your guest enjoyed their stay, and they tell others?

During turn-down service

Leave simple handwritten notes on the pillow such as *Sleep Tight* or *Sweet Dreams*.

Leave them with a last impression

Make certain they realize that you appreciate their business. An earnest *"thank you"* from you can go a long way. Give them a little memento from your property or region to take home with them as a lasting reminder.

Walk them outside

When your guests have checked out, walk them out the door, like you would do with close friends when they are leaving your home. A warm smile and a handshake can go a long way to encourage guests to return.

Alright, you have earned the right to ask for a referral by *WOWING* your guests, the next step is to ask for the referral.

You can do this by outright asking or by being more subtle

1. Ask your guests for feedback. Don't assume your guests are completely satisfied -ask. Rectifying a problem might allow you to shine and leave a favourable imprint if addressed positively.

2. This is an opportunity to exceed expectations. Personal feedback will always win over a comments form or questionnaire. Enquire about what they liked and what disappointed them; you can always learn and continue to improve.

3. You could ask them if they have any new ideas or for their recommendations on how things could be better. Guests will be flattered if you ask for their thoughts.

4. Follow up with a simple personalized handwritten thank you note tailored to them a few days after their departure, with a mention of a referral. This will not only show your appreciation, but it will give them something to remember you.

5. Keep in touch. Stay in touch with them so that when they come to book again you are firmly fixed in their minds. As a function of your outreach, let them know what other activities you have going on or what is happening in your area. Utilize an email list as well as social media.

6. Reward their loyalty with exclusive bargains. Make your faithful guests feel special by setting up exclusive packages or deals. Once again, this will show your appreciation of their business, as well as possibly inspiring other bookings.

7. Think of the things that are of high value to your guests but affordable to you so you can give added value. Always look at a problem or complaint as an opportunity to go that extra mile to wow your guest. Make it difficult for them to ever think about

not coming back to you. It's all about affording guests a reason to return and to tell others about your property.

8. Offer time-bound referral bonuses. During an Email or newsletter campaign, promote the property package and include that if they get additional friends or family members to book, they qualify for a larger discount.

9. Have a referral form on your website that offers discounts or bonuses.

10. Be incredibly thankful. This seems obvious, but so many businesses forget about it. Unless your price point is very low, having someone on your team place a call, send a handwritten note or send a gift for a referral is almost always worth it.

11. You can announce that you love referrals in your email signature and voicemail, so that every time a customer contacts you, they are reminded that you love referrals.

The bottom line is to talk, stay in touch and listen to your guests.

6. Negative Reviews Are Good For Business

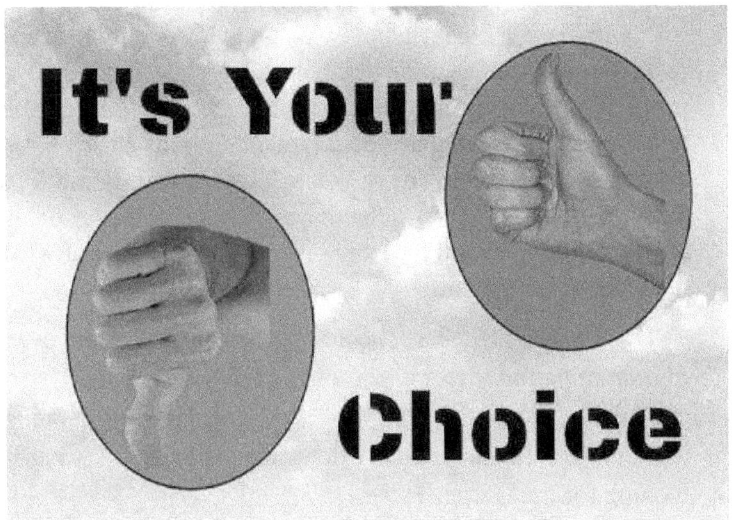

I don't care what a business you're in if you're dealing with the public, there are times you're going to get negative reviews and there is very little you can do. The choice lies in what you do with them. You can cover your ears, close your eyes and hope they go away, but unfortunately, with the Internet, that is never going to happen.

Take a look at these statistics from statisticbrain.com.

- *Number of travel bookings made on the internet each year — 148.3 million*
- *Percent of all travel reservations made on the internet — 57 %*
- *Percent of same-day hotel reservations made from a smartphone — 65%*

These statistics show that is vitally important for hospitality properties to have a strategy in place to find out what guests are saying when leaving a review.

I should make it clear right now that any hospitality property owner hoping to monitor every possible review about their property is in for a very difficult time since almost every online travel agency has feedback or comment sections about properties. Instead of driving yourself crazy, you should focus on a couple of the larger sites that have leverage in the hospitality and travel market, and they can give you a good idea of what is being said on other sites.

TripAdvisor is the largest site in the industry, having over 75 million impartial reviews, photos, and advice on hotels, attractions, restaurants, and vacations. This makes it the most influential and quite often the first site people look at when looking for travel advice.

Other sites that hold influence in the industry are those that provide booking services.

Orbitz

Travelocity

Expedia

They are important because they have a large number of users and a negative review could make a potential customer choose another property.

You have to monitor social media. A bad review on Facebook or Twitter can take off in no time and within days be on tens of thousands of timelines.

The last type of review site that you should stay aware of is the travel guides. Fodors and Frommers should be at the top of your list but as mentioned earlier in the book, more often than not, feedback in these types of publications would come from experienced staff.

I have heard *"A couple of bad reviews won't hurt my business, I can offer discounts."*

Research has shown that a slowdown in bookings due to bad reviews cannot be countered with discounts. At least not enough to recover the lost original business.

6.1 What can you do?

Encourage your guests to fill out your survey

Surveys can guide the respondent to consider the entire experience, not just the one thing that stood out when it comes to filling out a review or comment online. Guests who have a problem write a review about it 22% of the time. Guests without a problem write reviews just 9% of the time.

Encourage your customers to leave positive reviews

The simple fact is that customers are much more likely (maybe up to seven times) to leave a negative review or opinion. You need to be proactive in getting people to leave positive reviews and comments. If your customers say something nice to you then ask them to put it online. At the point of check-in and check-out, ask your customers to leave positive feedback.

Don't ignore negative feedback

As I mentioned earlier, you can't be perfect all the time, but you need to have an easy process in place for guests to leave both positive and negative reviews about your property. Engaging with the complaint in a clear, polite and positive fashion creates a

much more favourable impression with potential customers than
simply doing nothing.

6.2 How can negative reviews be good for business?

They give you authenticity

When you check out a business and see nothing but flattering
reviews and five stars, do you believe they're all true? Or is there
a little voice in the back of your brain saying to you *"This might
be too good to be true."*

It is possible to pay for good reviews or a hospitality property
owner could get their family to write them. Nothing is perfect
and because we are human, we all make mistakes.

If I'm looking at hospitality property reviews and I see a large
number of great reviews and a couple of not-so-great reviews, I
will take the time to look a little further. We all have days where
we can miss a hair in the sink or scrambled eggs are too cold and
if I see this type of thing written up in the review, I don't get too
worried.

You recognize (fixable) weak points

As a business owner, this is valuable information so you know
what needs to be fixed.

Negative reviews help your business to improve by showing
you areas where you can do better. Instead of fearing these types
of reviews, welcome them as an unfiltered look into your
business. Once you know where there's a problem or areas where
customers were confused, you can resolve the problem and make
the experience better for everyone. Instead of fearing these

comments, thank the people who leave them and tell them how you're going to change things for the better.

Let your customer service skills shine

If your customer takes the time to let you know what or where you can do better, thank them. This is valuable information. It also gives you a chance to show off your customer service skills, while giving others who are checking out your property the opportunity to see how much you value your customers.

Potential customers can tell a lot about a property by how they respond to criticism. If you handle the situation with grace, maturity and (when appropriate) humour, it tells them you're a business that is confident in what you offer and how you treat people. If you get defensive or argumentative, it tells potential customers you're a business they may want to avoid. It is important to respond wisely.

You give your loyal guests a chance to respond

If your property has received a negative review and you feel is unfair or undeserved, show it to some of your best and most loyal guests and ask what they think. If they feel the review is justified, they'll tell you and then you can correct the problem. If they don't, they're likely to go respond to that comment for you and help set the record straight. In many cases, if loyal customers feel you were wronged, they will come to your defence and be support for your brand.

If treated right, guests can be passionate about the people and properties they frequent. If they see someone talking badly about their hotel, resort, inn or bed and breakfast, they're going to jump into that conversation and fight for you.

You can change the conversation

As much as no one likes to see negative comments left about their property, they do give you the chance to change the conversation and that person's experience. By responding maturely, validating the critique, and offering a promise to do better, you can significantly increase someone's impression of your brand. And, truly, if someone is not happy with your service, don't you want to improve and make it right?

Reviews are important and the more positive reviews you have, the more likely it is a new customer will feel comfortable taking a chance on your business. Negative reviews also have their place and can offer some benefits to any business.

I have heard many hospitality property owners and managers tell me they don't have the time to search online for negative reviews about their property. Well, if you're only getting a few so-so negative reviews, you can probably live with that but, if you're getting reviews that are damaging your image and not dealing with them, it can have a major negative impact on your business.

If you cannot do this yourself, it is worth taking the time to give this task to a trusted employee or invest in *Online Reputation Management* or *ORM* company. If your property profile is stained with negative reviews, much of the time and money you are investing will go to waste, but with patience and caring, you can turn these around to your benefit.

7. How To Prepare For When Guests Return

Chances are when you open your doors to the world, guests are not going to be filing in. You're going to have to earn their trust.

If you look out your window, will you see brontosauruses or triceratops wandering around — no. Why? When the asteroid hit they were not able to adapt. In the last year and a half, Covid-19 has been a hospitality property mass extinction event and if properties didn't or are not willing to adapt, they will not survive.

7.1 How to get guests to trust you

Speak to any hospitality property owner or manager, and they will tell you the turmoil that they have been facing.

- *When should we open?*
- *When will our guests start returning?*
- *How do I forecast occupancy for the next 6 months, 12 months, 5 years with so much uncertainty?*
- *Is my business safe?*

It's no secret that the hospitality industry has taken a massive hit in the chaos that was 2020/21 but if you look closely, you can see a light at the end of the tunnel.

7.2 What are the signs?

People are tired of being stuck in a lockdown, and vaccine distribution is ramping up.

Currently, the Centers for Disease Control and Prevention is still advising against travel, but indicators already show travel is set to play a pivotal role in the widely predicted 2022 economic boom.

Travel set to make a gradual comeback but it will be different and if you haven't done so yet, it is time to start preparing.

7.3 How do we know people are getting ready to travel?

Many have been researching for travel inspiration for the past year as something to look forward to once vaccinated. A Booking.com survey from October 2020 that polled more than 20,000 people around the world found that 95% of respondents were spending free time looking at travel inspiration, with 38% looking at potential destinations at least once a week. 65% of respondents were excited about travelling in the future.

7.4 The tide is turning

The hospitality industry has been through the worst year in its history, however, better times are right around the corner. What you do now will determine how quickly your property will encounter recovery. Getting your team focused on existing business, new opportunities and how to protect, capture and grow that business will serve you well today and into the future.

How can hospitality properties up their game to attract these eager travellers? It may come down to revised safety & security procedures, some careful marketing and comparing your hospitality property to your market.

You need to take action or you *will* be left behind.

Is your hospitality property on the move?

If your property is open and it is doing as well as, or better than, the market, chances are you are doing things right. You probably have at least a small sales team or you are keeping up with what's going on around you. You mustn't lose this momentum. As we have seen throughout the past year, things turn on a dime.

Here are some takeaways for you to consider:

SWOT *(strengths, weaknesses, opportunities and threats)* analysis is your friend.

Now is the time to be brutally honest about your property compared to your competitors. It's important to remember in this process that you are likely competing with properties you might not consider as a competitor. Business is shifting across all segments. This is not the time to narrow your scope.

Analyze your business:

This will require both internal market segment reports and external business intelligence tools. You must understand what you have lost and what the market is capturing that you might be missing.

Assess what your property team is doing:

If they are doing something right, make sure you understand what it is and that they have the right tools to continue doing it.

Start playing the rate game:

It might be time to start the move upwards. This will jump-start your recovery and drive even more profitability.

Understand your market mix:

What is driving your impressive performance and how can you protect it? Make sure your property team keeps a close watch on each segment and has an action plan, not only to protect the business but also to grow it where possible.

Are you ready to recover?

If your property is ready to move forward, you have some work to do. The work stays the same even if you are in this situation and your market is in a different category.

Understand your market

If your market is outperforming you, what is driving their performance? If you have good business intelligence tools, you should be able to understand the market segment mix. Compare that to yours to find opportunities for your sales team.

Get your team moving

If your sales team is still involved in operational activities, it's time to curtail that. Your sellers need to be selling. Work with your team to pull together an action plan to start targeting business occurring in your market.

Be nimble

As your market shifts, new segments will appear. Be prepared to shift activity, spend, and do practically everything to capitalize on new opportunities.

What if you're still on hold?

Hospitality properties in this category may not be completely in control of their destiny. The takeaways for these properties will vary depending on the cause of the anxiety, especially if you are in one of the markets where COVID restrictions are still impacting performance.

The following are your best next steps:

Stay in touch:

Your past loyal guests need to know what is happening at your property. You'll have to make clear the murky waters of restrictions. Give them an understanding of where they'll be able to eat, what they can expect when out and about and what activities are available.

Prepare for reopening:

This doesn't just apply if your property is closed. If you are in an area with significant restrictions, having solid messaging for when things reopen will help you get the word out more quickly.

You should have cohesive messaging for email campaigns, as well as all social channels you use. This way when your property is ready to open for business, you can easily let everyone know.

Have staff available:

Even in regions with the heaviest restrictions, small meetings (within the guidelines) are happening. Those meetings are typically booked short-term and often in the same call inquiring about availability. During normal business hours, have at least one person who can handle those inquiries and book a meeting.

It's more important to understand where you stand.

7.5 Reviewing & revising, and adjusting

Getting the attention of those travellers looking to make up for the disappointments of 2020/21 will take a reassessment of accommodations and policies by hospitality property owners and managers.

Three major areas where properties can direct their efforts:

Safety and sanitation policies
Feature offerings
Overall room standards

Each of these categories can be a place for improvement and a source of guest attraction. As COVID vaccine rollout progresses, hospitality properties can review, revise, and adjust these hospitality components to draw in business

Sanitation and safety

Travellers in the modern era want to feel a sense of security and cleanliness they normally have to work hard to achieve.

Many hospitality properties have had success in reviewing their sanitation standards in light of the pandemic, but processes can always be improved. Drawing in guests in the foreseeable future, successful properties will have to ensure guests can distance themselves from others in clean environments. Consider methods to augment the sense of security and cleanliness of the property.

Walk-through security measures are one such feature that can provide a greater sense of safety in certain common areas. In the era of riots, civil tensions, and pandemics, such safety devices can help ease stress in guests.

Feature offerings

The pandemic forced a rapid shift to remote-work policies for millions of people. This is great news for the hospitality industry because it means a vacation no longer requires a full escape from work. Now, hospitality properties can appeal to spontaneous getaways that still make work possible, but this will require room accommodations and features to make such a getaway appealing.

Internet is everything. A fast Wi-Fi connection can be enough to draw in guests desperate for a change of scenery. Work-friendly stations within rooms are another great way to attract working visitors. Then, modern and exciting features like extended stay packages, flexible cancellation policies, and even robotic room service can solidify deals and get people out of their homes.

Room standards

In reviewing accommodations, it will help you to list out where improvements might be made and what modern trends could enhance guest experiences. While COVID challenges mean your budget likely won't allow for multi-million dollar renovations, there are plenty of smaller renovation projects you can take on to help your property stand out.

First off, start with a thorough review of needed maintenance on the property. A building maintenance checklist should include items like monthly, annual, and weather-specific maintenance tasks to check upon.

You can find a maintenance checklist in the resource section. Review all these items, then plan for improvements.

Rooms with smart and sustainable features like keyless entry and voice-activated controls will have greater appeal to spontaneous travellers. Touchless systems for check-in, check-out, and more will help travellers feel safe. Meanwhile, efforts to enhance privacy and guest distancing can improve the overall guest experience for the COVID era.

7.6 Embracing technology to effectively capture demand

Catching the attention of these travellers requires a more personal and tailored approach. Mass marketing and generic up-sells will no longer hit the mark; it's all about repositioning your services and fine-tuning your offering to meet the dominating needs of modern guests. From there, you can up-level your offering to something more attuned to their needs, reaching them with targeted email marketing, active social media promotion and curated up-selling via your internet booking engine.

7.7 Redefining your marketing strategy

Over the last year, guests have grown even more accustomed to fast technology, online communication and rapid responses, particularly during long stints of lockdowns, which means you'll need to keep your finger on the pulse to deliver at the pace they now expect.

7.8 Make a lasting impression across your social channels

Social media will be more significant than ever and is a key marketing channel for building trust and nurturing relationships with guests, both past and prospective. Make a positive impression by engaging with guests, answering queries.

7.9 You have to keep in mind

With pre-pandemic strategies now outdated and guests' needs continuing to fluctuate with changing travel conditions, creating and maintaining strong connections has never been more crucial.

A whole new era of travellers has emerged on the back of COVID, booking last-minute and domestic-fuelled getaways in quieter, crowd-free areas.

Staycation booms have been particularly noticeable in areas close to nature and beaches, with those that can travel feeling safer exploring locally than venturing internationally. Those who are no longer restrained by physical offices are using their remote freedom to take a 'workation,' seeking longer stays in properties that boast good views, stable internet, and homely amenities. Others are craving local experiences, free from tourists and off the beaten path.

Determine your target market and design your property to fulfil their needs, and you will be headed to recovery much sooner than later.

8. Reopening Hotels, Resorts, Bed and Breakfasts After COVID-19

What if I told you I could walk you through three stages for reopening your hotel, resort, bed and breakfast and how to use them to get you the other side of this pandemic?

Would you be interested?

What I'm going to share are creative, low-cost strategies to help hospitality properties acquire and retain customers. These are designed by system analysts who tend to be obsessive, curious and analytical:

- *These system analysts focus solely on strategies related to growing the business.*

- *They hypothesize, prioritize and test innovative growth strategies.*
- *They analyse and test to see what's working.*
- *The ideal system analyst knows how to set growth priorities, identify channels for customer acquisition, measure success, and scale growth.*

Each property is different and it's about figuring out why you grow and looking for ways to make that happen on purpose.

8.1 Defensive reactions

These are the immediate responses and adjustments you make for your business to survive. To slow down the bleeding and apply first aid. Aside from all the fiscal stuff your accountant should be telling you, by now you should have most of these in place. Examples are; rate and distribution modifications, inventory arrangement to demand, channel leveraging, front desk training, adjustments to your operation, so on and so on.

These items should by now be complete, or well on the way.

8.2 Tactical response

These are medium-term, the here and now. Making the best of a bad situation. Looking for the tactical actions you can take to keep the cash flow alive. Examples of what you can be doing right now include:

- *Adapting rates, conditions and finding new markets*
  Looking at self-isolation packages
- *Hosting medical staff*

- *Day rates for temporary offices*
- *Shift workers who can't return home between shifts.*
- *Considering new partners, new distribution and new ways of thinking.*

This will be a constant 'observe and act' approach until the crisis subsides.

Every head in a bed counts right now, and you need to ensure you're getting at least your fair market share.

8.3 Apparent opportunities

Once you've taken care of the immediate and medium-term priorities, now start to think like an entrepreneur, long-term. Be more creative; be more thorough. Get onto that project, review that technology upgrade, expand your footprint, and develop that market. You've likely never had so much time on your hands to work on your business, not in it. Much like a saying:
"When race car driver can't race, they work on their cars."
It's time to work on your car. But better than that, it is time to think of new ways to win races. It's time to optimize, time to recreate, time to re-imagine your business. Here's a handful of practical 'apparent opportunity' activities:

Online visibility audit

Taking a view of your hospitality property from your guest's point of view. Grab a laptop, a tablet and a smartphone and see what the booker sees when they have the desire to book a property in your area. Start with a Google search of your region. Check on multiple devices and follow the trail to the properties available. Pretend you don't know your property exists. Watch and learn;

- *How early does your property appear?*
- *How accurate a representation of your property is out there?*
- *Consider how it 'motivates' you to dig deeper?*
- *How easy it is to transact with your property?*

This activity will certainly uncover some areas for optimization.

Reading the future

The fact is, no one knows what the future will look like. Every hospitality property is unique and will need its approach to market demand returning. Therefore, the best way to create a customized approach, we believe, is to facilitate a planning session with your team. This activity is designed to help you arrive at a customized plan of attack, but one that potentially positions you well ahead of the marketplace and puts you on the front foot when demand returns.

Hospitality property health check

Take a more rounded view of your property comparing it against the industry. Your hospitality property health check should include occupancy, average rate & RevPAR along with all the online visibility factors like search, brand, website and social proof. It should also cover pricing, messaging, revenue management and sales strategy. This type of review helps to point out your areas of deficiency and maybe the action required to fix them.

Technology overhaul

Now is the time to consider an upgrade of your PMS, Channel Manager, CRM or perhaps some add-ons and enhancements to your existing technology stack. Only upgrade with features that will benefit your property. In other words, don't let technology lead your strategy. Use technology to leverage your strategy.

A roadmap

If you are going to re-invent yourself, you need a plan first. You not only need an *action plan* but an *execution plan* (a list of jobs to do, the order to do them and completion dates). Build yourself a plan, with thought, with strategic reason, and then follow through.

8.4 What do you need to do?

With so much information, both true and false, overloading our brains, many smaller owners and operators are struggling to find relevant information so they can put a return to operations plan in place that protects their guests and employees.

Paralysis by analysis is real, and now is not the time to fall victim to it. The following are outlines of actions that you can take today to make the reopening process more manageable.

Make sure it's manageable

You don't want to be overwhelmed. Divide your operations plan into its parts making it manageable.

Core job functions

Understanding the human resources you need and who will be responsible for what allows you to find and plan for gaps. You'll want to cover off on items such as:

- *Determining which roles and services should be excluded based on their risk of exposure*
- *Determining which roles need to be at your hospitality property & which can work from home during the pre-opening phase*
- *Making a list of work functions by date of return*
- *Outlining the new tasks that need to be covered by each job function and how that affects any furloughs or layoffs*

Property planning

You need to determine who will perform which task and where skills gaps exist, then the planning phase can begin. Here you should start to outline how your hospitality property will sell and occupy rooms / F&B spaces, and how guests and employees will interact. Items of particular attention include but are not limited to:

- *Outlining a room consolidation plan for a prolonged low occupancy period*
- *Determine COVID-19 employee training: Who, What When & Where*
- *Determine building entry and PPE requirements for employees and guests*
- *Determine plans/protocols for suspected cases: employees and guests*
- *Determine cleaning standards for high-touch areas and guest rooms*
- *Determine employee responsibilities related to self-administered practices to maintain health and safety*

- *Creating systems to verify and track that the health and safety plan is being followed*

Documentation

Documenting your plans for training and reference. The goal is to be able to provide effective training, ensure knowledge retention and create a system that is easy to reference when needed. In other words, updating your operations manual. Here, use the KISS formula (keep it simply simple). Find a balance between too much and not enough documented information.

Document property-specific SOPs established from the planning phase

- *Determine a COVID-19 Safety Plan. Note: Some jurisdictions require that you post your COVID-19 Safety Plan on your website — verify with your local authorities to see if you're required*
- *Complete a preparedness and response plan including readiness assessment and business continuity plan*
- *Establish vendor visitation policy and post it at vendor arrival points*

Communication

Communication takes several forms and must be tailored to your audience. From your hospitality property, you could be sharing information with owners, managers, guests, vendors, employees or the general public. Each will want to know specific details about items that impact them.

Those items are likely to include:

- *When you're re-opening, including F&B and other property amenities.*
- *Establishing your employee return to work policy for bringing the business back online*
- *Ensuring reservations and telephone operators have all necessary information to communicate cleaning practices and protocols to guests*
- *Sharing your COVID-19 safety, preparedness and response plans to multiple groups including local authorities if required*
- *Sending your new vendor delivery and visitation policy to all vendors*
- *Sharing traffic flow guidelines with guests before they arrive and during the check-in process*

Taking a logical, one step at a time approach to the planning and implementation of the process reduces the sense of being overwhelmed and emphasizes completing items before moving on to the next. This will allow you to feel organized and accomplished.

Not every hospitality property is the same so you have to look at these recommendations as a guide and should be adapted to your specific needs.

8.5 What is the next step?

Set a short period, three months, slow down and focus on what matters.

There's tremendous value in slowing down and dedicating the time to take stock of where you've been and where you're going; providing clarity for you and everyone who relies on your direction. Only after that can you put together a set of goals that will keep you and your team focused and prepared as soon as the *"new normal"* starts.

As your setting your goals, think back to some of your own experiences from the past year, talk with your employees and contact a few of your loyal guests to find out what would make them comfortable at your property. Look ahead and start thinking about new opportunities that are presenting themselves as a result of the new normal. Prioritize and stay laser-focused.

An 80/20 analysis is valuable here. In other words, where can you focus 20% of the work you do to generate 80% of the benefit. There is no need to put tremendous time and energy into a goal that won't yield beneficial results so make sure you're focusing on what matters and ignoring the rest.

Goals should motivate you

They should be important to you, benefit your property and you should be able to not only articulate them but show genuine excitement if you're sharing them with others. Goals should have milestones attached to them so that you not only know you're on track but so that you can celebrate the small victories along the way.

Your goals should be in writing

Writing down a goal that makes it feel real and concrete. It imprints on your brain and is hard to shake. Use action words like *"will"*, *"implement"*, *"demonstrate"* or *"solve"* instead of non-committal words like *"work on"* or *"would like"*.

Make an action plan

Document everything onto one sheet to get yourself focused.

Confirm opening or new property promotion date

If you're ahead of the game and have been able to set a re-opening date, your focus is less on immediate damage limitation and more on generating demand and revenue for your hospitality property. Here is the time you review your allocation strategy, making sure you're spending marketing dollars where they'll produce the most return, and get your message out to your ideal guests with alluring messages & attractive rates.

How to decide which guests to target, and with what rates

- *Ensure you have visibility of demand data for your market. Know who's searching, and for what.*
- *Refer to your historical data to set rates for the domestic short-stay market (those likely to return first).*
- *Calculate the likely value of different segments and price accordingly. Don't panic-drop rates.*
- *Monitor the industries being permitted to open back up in your local market. Pull lists of past corporate customers from those industries. Target them and companies like them.*
- *Reach out to your loyal members and/or previous guests with compelling offers on opening rates.*
- *If your audience has changed dramatically, focus on the most lightweight ways to engage that guest — targeted value offers and segmented messages.*

How to review your distribution strategy & position your direct channel to guests

- *Go back to your wholesale contracts and check they're watertight — no room for rate leakage.*

- *If considering new partners, test them out with sub-sections of inventory to see how they perform.*
- *Work out your margin on direct bookings and how you can use it to differentiate the channel vs OTA.*
- *Update content on all channels to reflect your opening, cleaning and safety policies.*

Directly before and after re-opening

When you're close to re-opening your doors to guests, issues of safety and guest satisfaction will be high on the agenda along with generating last-minute demand and optimizing your rates. This is where you need to be on top of things and making sure your key metrics are at least tracking towards their pre-COVID levels.

Guests may be travelling again, but this will not be travel as we currently know it — you'll need to be alert to fast-moving changes in legislation and behaviour and be prepared to change course as a result.

How to prepare your operations and implement new policies

- *Train returning staff on new housekeeping and guest management policies where relevant.*
- *Implement any physical changes at your hospitality property e.g. hand sanitizer stations; contactless check-in.*
- *Decide which areas of the property will re-open and how you'll distribute guests across rooms & floors.*

How to generate and convert demand

- *Reboot your marketing spend by opening back up your demand-generating campaigns.*

- *Highlight your cleaning and safety standards on your website and across your marketing channels.*
- *Try creative revenue drivers such as day rates for home workers or bundle offers for staycations.*
- *Keep a sharp eye on rate parity and which partners are delivering bookings. Be prepared to pause or cut off channels if the cost of sale is too high or their practices can't be trusted.*

How to prioritize guest satisfaction and safety
- *Make sure your cleaning standards are highly visible. Communicate with them on your property and online.*
- *Remove non-essential items from rooms, for example, magazines.*
- *Give upgrades to empty higher-rate rooms where possible.*
- *Reward bookers with instant rewards such as cashback or vouchers. Incentivize early guests to share their stays on social media to generate positive sentiment towards travel and your hospitality property.*

9. What Will Your Guests Expect Post Lockdown?

When faced with the challenge of preparing to reopen a hospitality property in an uncertain environment, it can be difficult to know where to start.

Where will potential guests travel from?
What will they want from their stay?
What can be done to increase demand?

9.1 Tailoring to post-lockdown guests

Part of a reopening strategy should include understanding who your post-lockdown guests are likely to be and what stay experience they are pursuing?

With ongoing international travel restrictions in place and public concerns about the safety of air travel, hospitality properties will likely see guests arriving from driving, rather than flying. Given corporate travel is pretty much at a standstill, properties should anticipate that the domestic leisure market will be a key focus for the foreseeable future.

Local leisure guests, who may travel as families, will understandably be cautious of putting themselves at an unnecessary risk after social isolation measures are eased, and as such properties need to provide services that make them feel secure and safe from public health standpoint. If applicable, hospitality properties should review their dining offerings to provide flexible options which allow for guests to enjoy meals in their rooms. This could include facilitating in-room meal deliveries from outside providers and provide a boxed breakfast doorstep delivery instead of the traditional buffet.

Guests will likely be more conscious of limiting interactions in common areas and will want to move through these areas quickly, with minimal contact.

Properties should provide either virtual, kiosk or contactless check-in procedures and be properly staffed to handle front desk needs quickly, avoid lines and overcrowding.

Cleaning and hygiene procedures are now at the top of the list as a desirable service for guests. Where once making cleaning shifts visible throughout the day was avoided by many properties, it should now be encouraged to increase the frequency of cleaning and make this visible to guests seeking reassurance of their safety. Hand sanitizers should continue to be made available at all guest contact points within rooms and in toiletry kits.

For upend or larger scale properties, boosted sanitation protocols could extend to sectioning off part of your property were not only enhanced cleaning measures are practiced, but where only guests and staff who have undergone on-site COVID-19 tests are permitted access.

Your communal-use areas like fitness rooms should set capacity limitations and allow guests to reserve equipment with thorough cleaning conducted between each use.

9.2 Recognizing a post lockdown recovery

Allowing that travel restriction will be a key factor in future guest demand. The observing of any changes to guidelines from the World Health Organisation, local infection control and government bodies is essential. The loosening or tightening of travel restrictions will directly impact a hospitality property's ability to attract guests in the future.

To aid with recovery efforts, properties should carefully monitor growth in their business by segment as well as a geographic source by the setting of benchmarks to better understand if guest demand is returning and at what volume. Identifying noteworthy forecasts for future months, plus understanding which segments are responsible for the upswing will help you to accurately identify and target potential business.

Daily analysis of booking trends and patterns is important. Government announcements are driving quick surges in demand with short lead-time bookings and cancellations. Forecasting these scenarios and strategically planning a revenue response is and will continue to be a significant contributor to a hotel, resort, inn or bed and breakfasts success.

9.3 Tactics for increasing demand

As regions prepare to reopen, individual properties should review not only government travel guidance and market conditions, but also your competitors.

The change in business mix and segmentation means your competitor set has changed and your product, guest experience and price positioning need to be re-evaluated. To accurately assess competitor pricing activity, you need to study their historical and current pricing to establish if your property matches up in price points. In some situations, you could have a far superior product at a price point similar to a competitor's basic room and adjusting pricing accordingly could help grow demand and steal share.

Hospitality properties can expect large uncertainty during the transition period as lockdown restrictions end. Customers will need more flexibility in case the situation changes again, and some may be fearful of committing to advanced booking with inflexible terms. The property's that offer and promotes greater booking flexibility will be more likely to obtain bookings in uncertain times.

Customers who book higher-priced accommodations such as suites are generally less price-sensitive, but that does not mean it will still be the case in the future. You have to be aware that it may be harder to achieve the same room category premiums, so consideration must be given to your strategy when it comes to inventory sharing and how you upgrade guests within your property. Many airlines are operating with low passenger numbers and offering upgrades for all passengers. This approach provides a great experience and promotes loyalty, which should be fostered in a low-demand market.

Flexibility in pricing, restrictions and inventory management is likely to extend past this transitional recovery period. For example, if there is not enough demand for premium room types but there is excess demand for standard rooms, it may be wise to overbook standard rooms and provide complimentary upgrades to normally higher-priced rooms. Understanding demand by room type and analysing this in combination with improving total hospitality property performance by using 'what if' modelling will enable property owners and managers to make informed, data-based decisions.

9.4 Fortify a profitable business

Reviewing the significance of existing pricing in the post lockdown 'new normal' and using data to make thoughtful pricing decisions that support short- and long-term strategies is crucial now more than ever. An automated revenue management system (RMS) enables properties to price competitively and confidently under any circumstance, including at times of exceptionally low demand.

While profits will take time to recover, the best opportunity to generate revenue efficiently is to ensure the seizure of the right business at the right price. In such circumstances, hospitality properties should use an RMS which evaluates future pace, price sensitivity, unrestricted demand, and even prices by room type and market segment to ensure they drive the most profitable business to their property.

9. 5 Be nimble in a fluctuating market

In times of uncertainty, it is difficult to predict a specific outcome. There will be plenty of time for historical review, but now is the time to purposefully plan, copy and prepare where you can, and to ensure your guests, employees and business are well protected in all aspects.

An agile approach to evolving market conditions and the ability to adapt to changing guest needs and business conditions will certainly help properties navigate a successful reopening.

9. 6 Design your property to prevent communicable diseases

Thinking about your interior design

We must treat communicable diseases as if it's our enemy and accept the fact that it will stay around for much longer than suits our lives. Redesigning hospitality properties to protect staff and guests will occupy owners and managers for the next many months or years, trying to rebuild trust and demonstrating that their property can be a haven to relax from the madness we are experiencing elsewhere.

So, what changes are possible or necessary to protect people from this 'enemy'? How far are we willing to go and what is acceptable by guests?

Pressure like this has always led to incredible creativity. One of the positive side effects of COVID-19 is that leads to new opportunities in the market. If interior decorators, hotel developers, architects and hospitality property management could help control the spread by introducing sophisticated interiors and reinventing properties, what would that be?

9.7 Ways to enhance safety

Personal hygiene at restaurants

COVID-19 is creating new requirements for safety, taking changes to restaurants or restaurant-style venues into account.

Washing hands before entering food serving areas is one of the challenging aspects that is forcing industry leaders to rethink existing designs. Some have already come up with innovative ideas, encouraging guests to wash their hands and make it a part of the dining experience. It is paramount to provide hand-washing facilities that include clean running water, liquid soap and paper towels. One possible idea is to locate stylish washbasins with sensory water taps or hand hygiene stations at entrances.

Devising the energy flow

If you have a restaurant at your property, you should separate entry and exit points to minimize contact and mitigate the potential risk of cross-contamination. A designated exit in restaurants will help to prevent confusion and convey the right message — a small detail that can make a big difference in COVID-19 safety. Signage, barriers and communication with guests remain key!

Interior fabrics

The coronavirus has caused interiors to be set up a certain way to lessen the overall risk. It has changed the way hospitality properties and restaurants are now getting decorated using cleanable fabrics on upholstered furniture to keep people safe. Select materials that are easy to clean.

Common area social distancing

Consider social distancing measures for the layout of your seating areas in your foyer, F&B outlets, lounge and common areas. Many guidelines indicate that tables should be placed a certain way to ensure that persons seated at those tables are 1.5

metres or 6 feet (1.83 m) (minimum) apart. You may have to reduce the number of tables and the seating capacity to stay in line with public health directions. This can be implemented in very different ways, for example using potted plants, sculptures or elegant partition walls. Here you can use your imagination.

Floor markings

Social distancing measures must be visible. It has become a best practice to install floor or wall markings or signs to identify the distance between people for queues and waiting areas.

Tableware

Stop using tablecloths as it can lead to cross-contamination. More importantly, service staff should take extra precautions when providing cloth napkins (wearing gloves during folding and when removing dirty napkins etc.). The industry is now discovering that tablecloths must be finally removed from the inventory list, which follows the general trend of the bare table surface concept in gourmet restaurants.

Go contactless

Where practical, physical barriers should be installed, such as Plexiglas/or glass around counters involving high volume interactions with guests to protect service staff from COVID-19. Avoid touch screens where possible.

Hand sanitizer stations

There are already stylish integrated sanitizer stations that invite guests to try them out available. If hand washing facilities are not readily available, the property should provide an appropriate alcohol-based hand sanitizer. We can get used to seeing hand sanitizer stations throughout the entire property.

Elevators

Coronavirus has changed the way we ride elevators. The risk of cross-contamination in confined spaces, such as elevators, should be identified in the Risk Management Plan. Safety measures should be implemented for people using the elevators, such as limiting the number of people in the elevator at one time, providing hand sanitizer, and ensuring elevator buttons are cleaned frequently.

Near field communication (NFC)

NFC is an access control technology that allows guests to do things like open room doors with their smartphones. It took almost 10 years to find acceptance in the market, but thanks to COVID-19 the contactless access control technology now has another selling point.

Security checkpoints

Properties with luggage and guest screening at the entrance must also rethink the way security screening is conducted. Airports are already testing out new procedures to lessen the potential risk of cross-contamination. Key issues include the disinfection of trays, pat-downs and bag searches. However, under no circumstances should COVID-19 safety measures compromise security.

10. What Is The Future Of The Hospitality Property Industry?

The hospitality property industry is shifting.

In the last hundred plus years, with the invention of the automobile, the internet and today with the competition are coming from everywhere, customer behavioural changes are creating a shared economy. The big difference is that the world is moving faster than ever, with new technologies, economic and demographic changes, transforming social attitudes all driving the way we live, work and do business.

The core values of the hospitality property industry will stay consistent but if you are not willing to keep up with the times, you will not reap the benefits and possibly be left out in the cold.

10.1 What is the future?

Smart hotels

Smart hotels are properties that incorporate the *Internet of Things*. This is where a network of physical objects such as heating, ventilation, and air conditioning systems, or lighting and entertainment systems are embedded with electronics that enable the objects to provide greater value and service. As more and more people make use of smart technology in their homes, smart hospitality property rooms are likely to see higher demand. These devices and systems will streamline the day-to-day operation of the property, make things more efficient and improve guests' experience.

Other benefits to property owners and guests

More personalization

Greater personalization in hospitality property marketing makes customers feel appreciated, not just another anonymous statistic on the balance sheet. Targeting individuals with precise booking offers are more effective, and they are likely to buy.

This is great for repeat business.

A smart hotel also offers exceptional opportunities to deliver personalization. For example, TVs can be remotely set up to refer to guests by their name, while a central control point can be used by guests to set conditions within the room. The devices will then automatically create those conditions.

Information is more accessible

This means a guest could use their voice to ask a question and then receiving an intelligent answer. Devices can also be connected to other hotel services or the internet, allowing guests

to find information and reviews for local bars, restaurants and
tourist attractions.

Data-Driven Decision Making

As long as properties are transparent and follow data protection
legislation, some customer information obtained from smart hotel
solutions can be useful. While they will have to securely delete
customer voice commands, and other data from devices like
Amazon Echo, certain information can be collected, including
basic usage data.

Preventative maintenance & repairs

Customers and hospitality property owners can benefit from
the ability that a smart hotel provides for pre-emptive
maintenance and repairs. Staff will be able to see performance
information and operational data for specific devices, in real-time
allowing them to spot problems quickly, or even before they
happen, allowing repairs to be made earlier. As a result, fewer
guest disruptions, early repairs may save money on replacement
devices, and less money lost due to rooms out of service.

AI — Artificial intelligence

More and more businesses are using AI to handle some of their
customer services, with simple but powerful chatbots providing
support, fielding queries and even taking care of the entire
booking process. Artificial intelligence is one of the most
important hotel industry trends right now, transforming the sector
in subtle but important ways.

All hospitality properties of the current and future generation
significantly need a connected platform and ecosystem that is
constantly acquiring, contextualizing, processing and analysing

customer data, and turning it into predictive and actionable insights for generating an excellent guest interaction and experience. AI will enable properties to leverage all the data coming from across the front to back offices, then translate and harness all of this unstructured and disparate data into accessible smart perceptions in a cost-effective way.

Virtual reality

Virtual reality is becoming an established part of everyday life.

Virtual reality or VR is a computer technology, which uses images, sounds and physical sensations to make users feel as though they are physically present in a virtual world. VR can also be very useful for customers who want to explore their destination before they commit to a trip. They are becoming a very powerful marketing tool, giving customers a chance to stroll around a property to experience some of its features before they visit. VR hotel tours have become an important hotel industry trend.

AR — Augmented reality

Augmented reality is a close cousin to virtual reality.

Where virtual reality replaces the real world with audio and visual input to create an immersive experience, augmented reality simply adds virtual elements to the real world. This could mean, for example, a smartphone app that displays listings, opening times and other information over the business or attraction that a visitor is looking at.

Hospitality properties can use AR to provide interactive maps and information about services such as spas, gyms, restaurants etc. Hotels are also using AR games to make their guests' visits more enjoyable and memorable.

Sustainability

Hospitality property sustainability is not only about going green and saving the planet. It's focusing on overall good.

Sustainability has become one of the more popular industry trends, as today's environmentally conscious customers demand choices that are in line with their ethics. At the minimum, modern consumers often require that their property of choice is as energy-efficient as possible.

Here are a few examples of what others are implementing in their properties:

- *Support local sources*
- *Use LED bulbs and install sensor based lights in the common areas*
- *Hire locally. This reduces local unemployment rates*
- *Properties near a forest — promote reforestation.*
- *Properties near the seaside, the "Eco-Pure" system. It purifies seawater and makes it to drinking water*
- *Recycle glass bottles & reduce or stop consumption of plastic bottles*
- *Solar panel roofs. It can power the AC in hot places and be a great heating source in the cold season. They will also lower your carbon imprint.*

- *An organic garden. It can be a smaller one for herbs or a much larger one which can produce vegetables for your property's kitchen.*

- *The use of eco-friendly cleaning products*

- *Refillable shampoo or shower gel containers*

- *Bicycles for guests as an alternative transportation*

- *Use rainwater for garden or plant watering*

- *Recycle used toiletries for communities in need*

- *Use all data in the system — saves paper*

Robots

More and more hospitality properties are incorporating robots in some capacity or another. Building a positive memory is a must for hospitality property owners or managers. They want the guest to leave, share that experience with others and then return.

How can robots help with this?

Multiple hotel chains have been testing the use of robot technology to help with this for several years now and the consensus is that it provides a competitive edge over their competitors who have chosen not to try. Robots have the potential to free up the time of human staff and assist in the personalization of a guest's stay. And that is just to start.

Their use is almost limitless, with only imagination, and the cost, limiting faster development.

Old fears will become a new motivation

The growth of Airbnb and similar companies will not be viewed as huge threats. Things are changing to a traditional hospitality properties benefit.

Here's what's happening:

- *Pressure from Airbnb and other competitors has pushed hoteliers towards better practices by embracing a more creative and unique experience for their guests.*

- *As Airbnb continues to expand, properties are expected to expand into more home-sharing, which means more opportunities for profitability.*

- *71% of a traveller survey said they believed that hospitality properties still have an edge over Airbnb in terms of cleanliness, advertised "authentic" experiences, and location options.*

Property owners have to face the fact that home-sharing isn't going anywhere but by working in tandem with hoteliers, services like Airbnb is providing more flexibility to group sales strategy or, depending on your location, paving the way for your own better versions of offerings.

Combining business & leisure travel

Millennials tend to be a fairly thrifty demographic with both, a work hard, play hard approach to life. These traits have driven bleisure (business/leisure) travel.

Combining business and work with leisure travel, bleisure travel represents the best of both worlds. Extending a work trip to take advantage of a destination or just squeezing in a little sightseeing before or after work. Millennials are finding practical ways to explore the world without taking time off work.

Health and well-being top-of-mind

Travellers are becoming more health-conscious, and wellness travel has seen an increase in recent years. Technology is helping people keep a closer track of their health, with many apps and devices providing daily, even minute-by-minute updates on blood pressure, sleep, calories etc.

This might include changing a hotel restaurant's menu, upgrading amenities, putting on classes, or renovating rooms to give guests the freedom of choice they want. What binds all these trends together is the combination of personalization and data. The better you know your market, the more precise your offering can be to make each customer happy.

Now you understand what your guests expect, what's your next step?

If you have not seen the three other books in the series, Pick them up.

"Hospitality Property Organizational Structure" book

"Steps To Hiring Exceptional Hospitality Property Staff" book

"Marketing Strategy for Hospitality Property's" book

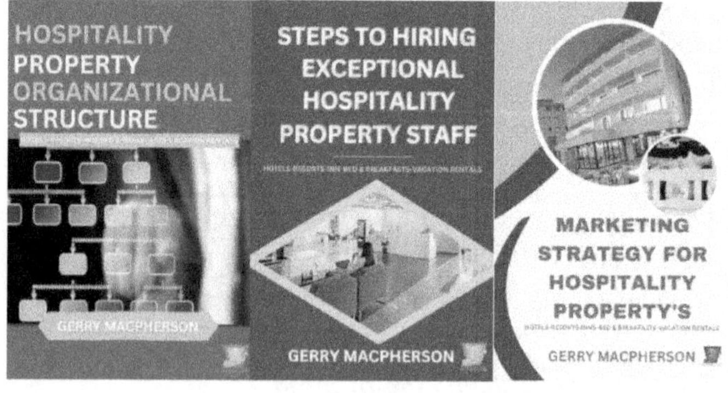

What's Next …

Operating a Successful Hospitality Property
Just Got Easier…

You're just a heartbeat away from the crucial training, advice & support you need to plan, create & grow a prosperous and rewarding, hotel, resort, inn, bed and breakfast or vacation rental.

Does any of this sound familiar?

- *You have a great idea for a hospitality property, but don't know where to start and how to turn that into a real plan...*

- *You've spent countless hours working your business but your organizational structure is lacking and you're tired of having to do everything yourself...*

- *Your employees are not living up to your standards and the good ones leave...*

- *Your marketing is not working as it should and you're not reaching your target audience...*

- *You feel you're a step or two behind your competition...*

If any of these things ring true, then you already know what a minefield it can be trying to get quality advice & support.

Introducing the Hospitality Property School Group

We are travel authorities that have spent 1000's nights in properties of all classes worldwide, conducting countless site inspections for several world-class tour companies, as well as received feedback from 100,000's of guests.

This knowledge has given us a unique insight into the wants, needs and requirements of individual and group travellers, as well as management and employees.

We provide strategies for, and aid in the growth and development of hotels, resorts, inns and bed & breakfasts to create their brand and goals; as well as increase their bookings and profit while keeping their integrity.

The Hospitality Property School Group is packed with in-depth, practical training and resources on all aspects of planning, building, running and growing a successful hospitality property.

Here is How You Will Benefit:

Actionable Workbooks

Actionable workshops are a series of short mini-courses that you can study and then utilize the best practices for your business.

Courses

The design of the courses is the result of decades of experience that have given us insight into the wants, needs & requirements of hospitality property guests, management & employees.

Resources/Perks

You have access to the free resources download centre designed to help streamline your organizational structure, grow your bookings & increase your bottom line. As a member, you deserve a break. Keystone HPD has created a number of training tutorials, ebooks, audiobooks & video production opportunities and you can SAVE up to 50%.

Member Properties

What makes your property special? Tell us about your property, your region, your success stories, your great employees, your favourite guests. Every month we'll pick our one to highlight on the group site.

Q & As

Do you have a question? Ask them here and let the experts in our community share their thoughts, tell their stories & best practices. In this section, we'll catalogue the best responses.

Community Voice

Have you had any game-changing ideas? Tell us in the "Community Voice" section and we'll share the ones we like here and in the monthly update.

You'll Also Find Material on The Following Topics:

- Your Guests
- Personal/Employee Development
- Facility
- Marketing
- Hospitality Property Checklists

- Trends
- Technology
- Operations Manual Development
- Interviews
- Webinars
- Ted Talks
- *INN*sider Tips
- Podcasts

The Hospitality Property School Podcasts provide strategies & techniques to aid in the growth & development of hospitality properties while increasing patronage & profit.

Within the group, you'll have the opportunity to ask questions, share best practices, promote your property etc.

Plus, be able to watch the training tutorials, the video podcasts and listen to the interviews when it fits into **your** schedule.

This is your group and we want you to benefit to the fullest.

WHAT MAKES THE HOSPITALITY PROPERTY SCHOOL GROUP SPECIAL?

ACCESS TO EXPERTISE

Tap into our decades of experience in the industry.

NO B.S. ALLOWED

We're not into overblown hype, marketing tricks or jumping on the latest shiny bandwagon. Just straight-talking, honest, proven and practical advice. No B.S. or tricks!

OUR FULL COMMITMENT

We eat, sleep and breathe the hospitality property industry. The group is our main focus and we love helping our group members achieve success. It's what we do, and we're not going anywhere!

Are you ready to take your property to the next level?

Get Instant Access to the Hospitality Property School Group!

https://member.keystonehpd.com

In case you were wondering, we have a

14 Day No Questions Asked Money-Back Guarantee

When you join the Hospitality Property School Group, you are fully protected by our 100% Satisfaction Guarantee. If you don't feel like you've received value and you decide you want to cancel any time within the next 14 days, just let us know and we'll send you a prompt refund. No hassles, headaches or hoops to jump through. We're confident that you'll find the Membership Academy useful, and we won't make you beg or invoke any silly rules or conditions - if you're not satisfied within your first 14 days then we'll refund you without any fuss.

Simply copy & click the link for your payment option to join

https://member.keystonehpd.com